C000112973

Routemasters IN COLOUR

Geoff Rixon

Ian Allan
PUBLISHING

Familiar Pattern

Front cover: As will become all too evident in the pages of this book, LT carried out a massive cull of Routemasters around 1985 and RM495, seen here coming off Westminster Bridge into Parliament Square, was one of the victims. However, this one avoided scrapping for five years by moving to Clydeside Scottish and then to Western Scottish. Here we see the vehicle at its best on 5 September 1981, fresh from overhaul at Aldenham Works. *Geoff Rixon*

Reaching the Top

Back cover: It is October 1998 and here is a Routemaster in regular public service, in the peak of condition. This splendid vehicle, RM1214, is wearing vintage Halifax livery, based on Glasgow colours and is complete with rear-wheel dustbin lids. Formerly in the LT Reserve Fleet, this is one of the four Routemasters operated by Halifax Joint Committee and is seen ascending the hill from Sowerby Bridge into Sowerby. *Malcolm King*

Better Late Than Never

Title page: The future prospects of the 1954-built pioneer Routemaster looked bleak when it was sold in 1972 to Lockheed Hydraulics, and even on its subsequent repurchase by LT, when it languished in the dip at Chiswick Works. However, fortune finally smiled on RM1 in 1982 when it was refurbished by the apprentices at Aldenham Bus Overhaul Works and donated to the LT Museum. This rare picture shows the vehicle, soon after refurbishment, specially posed between the reservoirs at Walton-on-Thames in May of that year. Perhaps one day funds will be found to reconstruct the original front end. *Geoff Rixon*

First published 1999

ISBN 0 7110 2682 3

All rights reserved. No part of this book may be reproduced or transmitted in any form or by any means, electronic or mechanical, including photocopying, recording or by any information storage and retrieval system, without permission from the Publisher in writing.

© Geoff Rixon 1999

Published by Ian Allan Publishing

an imprint of Ian Allan Publishing Ltd, Terminal House, Shepperton, Surrey TW17 8AS. Printed by Ian Allan Printing Ltd, Riverdene Business Park, Hersham, Surrey KT12 4RG.

Code: 9909/C

Introduction

Welcome to *Routemasters in Colour*, a companion to *The Heyday of the Routemaster*, published in 1997 and subsequently reprinted.

The earlier book traced the life of the celebrated Routemaster bus from the introduction into service of the prototype, RM1, in 1956 through to Reading's expanding fleet in 1996.

Now that 40 years have elapsed since the first production Routemasters entered service, another colour album seems appropriate. However, in order to distinguish the new book from its predecessor, coverage is confined to the last 20 years, 1979-99 and, London apart, different vehicles and liveries have been featured as much as possible, both at home and abroad. For simplicity, London Transport (LT) fleet numbers have been used throughout.

The Routemaster fleet in London has not greatly altered since 1996. There are still nearly 500 RMLs and close on 100 standard-length RMs in regular service. The main change has been in Routemaster operations outside London. Apart from the few used for sightseeing, and other tourist duties and the occasional one-off, the only ones in regular passenger services are limited to Reading, where there are 26 licensed, and Halifax which has four. Consequently, virtually all the provincial liveries featured in this book are now part of history.

Despite all the scare stories in the media about the demise of the London Routemaster, some routes have just been retendered and been accepted for further Routemaster operation and it is clear that the class will be in service well into the new millennium. Indeed, following the modernisation of the RMLs in 1993, more and more standard RMs are being updated, with new Scania engines being fitted. There are very few still running with their original AEC engines.

As living proof of the longevity of the remarkable Routemaster, on the day these words are being written (12 March 1999) the first production Routemaster to be delivered, RM6, which reached LT on 11 May 1959, and the last standard-length Routemaster to be built (RM2217) have both been seen operating on Route 159. It is an amazing feat of design and engineering that these old warhorses are still worth having money spent on them, to keep them in front-line service into the next century.

Acknowledgements

In compiling this second colour album I would like to thank several photographers for supplying their high-class colour material for which I am very grateful: Malcolm King, Colin Brown, Andy Izatt, Vernon Murphy, Mike Harris, Andrew Morgan, Trevor Muir, Dave Brown, Philip Lamb, Chris Morrison, Mark Bailey and Billy Nicol.

Grateful thanks also to Kevin McCormack for many invaluable hours spent helping with the photographic selection and writing of the text, also to Alan Stokes for word processing the result.

As regards information and research, I was greatly assisted by Capital Transport's *Routemaster Handbooks by* Andrew Morgan.

I hope you will enjoy this second album and see many more years of Routemaster operation.

Geoff Rixon
April 1999

Growth Industry

Left: When this photograph was taken in August 1997, Reading Mainline was still increasing its Routemaster collection, purchasing the former Blackpool Transport fleet in that year, including this resplendent addition, RM1627, which became No 38. The Reading contingent has now reduced, following the takeover by Reading Buses but is still by far the largest RM operator outside London, with 26 vehicles still licensed for service. *Geoff Rixon*

Heritage Livery

Right: This view at Mansfield garage, in the summer of 1989, shows RM1164 shortly after its transfer from Magic Bus of Glasgow. East Midlands had promptly reregistered the vehicle and applied the company's much loved early livery as seen here. The bus left East Midlands in October 1992 for Stagecoach Perth and then Bluebird Buses. Readers wishing to see what RM1164 looked like when it was a brand-new trolleybus replacement vehicle are invited to view the cover of the author's previous volume *The Heyday of the Routemaster. Malcolm King*

Shopping Around

Above: In 1979 16 RMs were painted in the distinctive livery shown here for use on a circular service which linked various well-known West End stores. All the vehicles worked out of Stockwell and carried sponsor's advertising. This view of RM2207 was taken at Hyde Park Corner on 14 April 1979, one week after the operation commenced. Due to lack of patronage, Shoplinker ceased on 28 September the same year and the vehicles reverted to red livery. In 1988 RM2207 was overhauled by LT for Sri Lanka Transport Board and duly exported. *Colin Brown*

Country Life

Right: This former Green Line coach, which started its working life at Epping in October 1962, became one of London Country's last Routemasters, remaining in service until February 1980. This view dates from 29 August 1979 and depicts RMC1483 standing outside Dartford garage, looking remarkably smart compared with other surviving Country Routemasters. After sale to LT the vehicle was used as a trainer until August 1989. Shortly afterwards it was scrapped at Wandsworth garage. *Colin Brown*

5

Goodbye to Green

Below: This view, taken at Warren Street on 12 April 1980, shows RML2336 wearing red livery for the first time. New to Godstone in November 1965 and transferred to London Country on 1 January 1970, the vehicle was repurchased by LT along with all the surviving green Routemasters (except RMC4) following the end of crew operation. This vehicle is still in service today, with London Central. *Geoff Rixon*

Sunday Service

Right: Given that all the shops would have been closed, there are a remarkable number of people trying to board RM1384 at Liverpool Street on the day of rest, in this case Sunday 10 August 1980. Seven years later the bus had lost out in the popularity stakes and was made redundant; it now serves as a bar in Tokyo, Japan. *Geoff Rixon*

Northern Delights

Left: This fortunate bus, seen here in spring 1980 at Crook, County Durham in its final livery, was purchased for preservation a few months later and has been repainted in its original colours. No 3089 was one of 50 unique front-entrance long Routemasters, purchased new by Northern General. It also acquired, second-hand, the former LT demonstrator RMF1254, of similar configuration. *Dave Brown*

No Expense Spared

Right: In 1980, LT took the unusual step of undertaking major alterations to 40 long Routemaster coaches repurchased from London Country, and put them to work on the 149 route out of Stamford Hill and Edmonton. Whether the investment was worthwhile for their four years of service in the role is debatable but they certainly caught the imagination of bus enthusiasts by providing added variety to London bus operations. This view shows RCL2223 at Victoria on 18 August 1980, eight days after RCL operation commenced. Following disposal by LT, the RM has passed through several hands and is currently owned by AVS Graphics of Farnham, Surrey, who use it as a hospitality vehicle. *Geoff Rixon*

Over the Border

Left: Uxbridge was unusual for being a Central Area (red buses) garage but technically located in the Country Area, beyond the Greater London Council boundary (although the town was within the boundary). The garage provided some of the vehicles for the well-established 207 route to Shepherd's Bush (formerly tram Route 7 and trolleybus Route 607). One of its 1980 residents was RM29, photographed at Hayes End on 16 December. Reregistered OYM 453A in 1988, the vehicle was withdrawn by MTL in March 1998, when Route 139 was converted to one-person-operation, and added to the LT Reserve Fleet.
Geoff Rixon

Dream Ticket

Above: With a backdrop more reminiscent of the French Riviera than Hyde Park Corner, RM1737 heads not for Monte Carlo but Hammersmith on 16 April 1981. This Dalston garage Showbus was privileged to be selected for preservation by the LT Museum following its withdrawal from service in April 1985.
Geoff Rixon

Out of Season

Spring may be bursting out all over Surbiton but RM92 was in the autumn of its
life when photographed on 17 April 1982 in Upper Brighton Road. This bus was
scrapped at Carlton, a little over three years later, a victim of the conversion of
Route 71 to one-person-operation in August 1985. *Geoff Rixon*

12

Sad Ending

RM561 was chosen, with seven others, for repainting in a special livery to celebrate the wedding of HRH The Prince of Wales and The Lady Diana Spencer on 28 July 1981. Selected to operate on certain cross-London routes over the summer and early autumn, this vehicle was photographed, on 7 July 1981, entering Hyde Park Corner from Grosvenor Place, with the boundary wall of Buckingham Palace behind. Unfortunately, less than four years after the wedding, RM561 was going to its own funeral. *Geoff Rixon*

Last Overhaul

Left: RM582 of New Cross travels along Whitehall in July 1981 in ex-works condition. Exactly four years later it was withdrawn at New Cross and sent to a breaker for scrapping. *Geoff Rixon*

Lovely Sheen

Right: RML2645, looking resplendent after its recent visit to Aldenham Works, travels along the Upper Richmond Road, Sheen, on Route 37 in August 1981. The bus is still in service today, working for London United Busways out of Shepherd's Bush garage and now has a Cummins engine. *Geoff Rixon*

Wrong Choice

Above: Streatham garage, opposite which RM1441 is standing, might have done better by not choosing a Leyland-engined Routemaster for its Showbus because these were favourites for early withdrawal. Less than two and a half years after this view was taken in August 1981, the resplendent vehicle was sold to a scrap merchant. *Geoff Rixon*

No Tourists Here

Right: RM90 has been operating on London Sightseeing Tours since 1986 but this particular part of Stratford is unlikely to have been featured in the itinerary. This view dates from April 1982 when the bus was operating from Leyton garage. RM90 was converted to open-top in 1986 and extended in length in 1990 by the insertion of an additional window bay and is now running as ERM90, working out of Wandsworth garage with Arriva. *Geoff Rixon*

One-Day Wonder

Left: This is Finchley on 18 June 1988. We are witnessing a unique working, when RML900 from Johnstone (J) garage, 400 miles away, is operating OPO Route 26. It was returning briefly to London on a guest visit, working from its original garage, Finchley (FY). Following severe frontal damage in 1987, LT sold the vehicle to Clydeside Scottish who rebuilt it, fitting a one-piece windscreen and DMS-style trafficators. In the process, RML900 became the only vehicle of this class to operate outside London. It was subsequently sold, in January 1995, to Blue Triangle of Rainham. After years in storage, it is currently being refurbished by the company.
Geoff Rixon

Going Dutch

Right: There are some unusual aspects to this photograph of RM545 taken near Brixton in 1988. The vehicle in question belonged to London Coaches of Wandsworth and was undertaking fuel evaluation trials, operating out of Victoria and, as seen here, Norwood garages. The reason for the trials was that RM545 had just been fitted with a DAF engine, the only Routemaster so treated. The bus remains part of the London Sightseeing fleet today.
Geoff Rixon

Hackney Carriage

Left: RM1251 shows off its new London Buses roundel at the well-known bus stand at Kensal Green. Although bound for London's East End in April 1988, this was clearly not far enough east for this vehicle's liking because three years later it was despatched to Japan! *Geoff Rixon*

Revolving Credit

Above: RM798 circles the plastic money signs at the Asda supermarket in Hull, in May 1988. The vehicle had just been purchased by East Yorkshire, from LT, in the previous month so is fresh from the paintshop. Sadly, it was to lose its registration two years later and is now numbered NRH 802A. It remains with East Yorkshire but in store. *Geoff Rixon*

Northenders

Left: Despite the marketing slogan carried by RM2114, this bus is operating in Lancashire, 200 miles north of Albert Square. One of four Routemasters purchased by Burnley & Pendle, RM2114 operated with that company for less than two years and was last recorded in Budapest, Hungary. This shot was taken in May 1988, two months after acquisition, when the vehicle looked magnificent in its smart new livery. *Geoff Rixon*

Burg(h)er Bus

Right: Having transported the burghers of London, Southampton and Southend for over 30 years, this vehicle is now associated with burgers of the edible kind. RM1682 is seen here in May 1988, working for Southampton Citybus during its three-year sojourn on the South Coast. The next three years found the bus on the east coast, No 117 in the Southend Transport fleet. Then in 1994 it was away to Germany for use as a McDonald's children's party bus. *Geoff Rixon*

Unusual Side Effect

Whatever it is that is found in all the right places, RM1821 ended up in the wrong place, a Dundee scrapyard, just two and a half years after this view was taken in Perth in April 1990. *Malcolm King*

South American Way

Exported to Argentina in 1998, RMA16 has had a varied life which shows no sign of coming to an end. New to BEA in December 1966 as No 14, the vehicle became an LT staff bus at Hounslow in November 1976 and was sold to Clydeside Scottish in November 1988. There it was renumbered SRMA1 and fitted with coach seats for excursion work (as seen here in Dundee on 12 May

1989). After eight years north of the Border, RMA16 ventured south again, being signed up by London & Country to replace RM1183 on special duties and received Lincoln green livery. After only a short time it was farewell Leatherhead and hello South America. *Colin Brown*

Culture Bus

Left: This photograph, taken at Old Kilpatrick in 1990, shows Kelvin Central's RM439 wearing all-over livery, to celebrate Glasgow as the European City of Culture and the Glasgow East End. Originally based at Hanwell on trolleybus replacement duties in November 1960, this vehicle moved north of the Border to Kelvin Scottish in March 1986. Sadly, it went for scrapping in November 1992.
Malcolm King

Extended Tour of Duty

Below: In 1986 LT converted 20 standard-length Routemasters into open-toppers for London Sightseeing duties and decided to increase the passenger capacity of half of the fleet by inserting an extra central bay. This created an additional full-size window in contrast with the half-size windows fitted to production RMLs. The 10 Routemasters were redesignated ERM and former RM163, which entered service at Walworth in February 1960, was photographed in April 1990.
Geoff Rixon

Gone for a Burton

Below: This well known biscuit manufacturer bought RM1123, in June 1987, from LT but sold it to Blackpool Transport in December 1989, only to repurchase it in April 1994. This photograph, taken at St Anne's-on-Sea, dates from April 1990 and shows the vehicle still wearing Burton's livery. *Malcolm King*

Touch of Class

Right: Another provincial operator to take pride in its Routemaster fleet by adopting a striking traditionally based livery was Blackpool Transport whose RM1583 is seen here at St Anne's-on-Sea in April 1990. The Blackpool fleet lasted for over 10 years and was sold en masse in 1997 to Reading Mainline. *Malcolm King*

Secret Service

Below: When Haven Coaches of Newhaven acquired RM933 in June 1991, it was a case of a quick repaint and then out on to the road, leaving no time to apply the operator's name on the sides. Under stormy skies but in the right area to find a safe haven, RM933 displays its smart new blue and white livery, contrasting with its previous LT and Clydeside Scottish colours. *Malcolm King*

Just the Ticket

Right: Green Rover, affectionately remembered by former bus spotters as their passport to visit the extremities of LT's Country Area, was the name adopted by a Watford operator. Here we see RMA14, formerly BEA No 2 and later an Aldenham staff bus, working a local service for that operator in April 1991. *Malcolm King*

Leap into the Unknown

February 29 1992 was the first day of London Coaches' takeover of former Green Line Route 726 and to celebrate the occasion RCL2260 was used on a return trip from Heathrow to Croydon, pausing here at Hampton Court. Made redundant by London Country in March 1979, this vehicle was repurchased by LT and refurbished for operation on Route 149 from Edmonton garage. RCL2260 is now with Arriva and still operates in London. *Geoff Rixon*

Memories

Reduced in height in preparation for travelling to Germany in June 1992 to promote the musical *Cats*, RM1181 stands outside an opening in Fulwell garage through which one half expects to see a tram or trolleybus still lurking. *Geoff Rixon*

What a Star!

Left: This bus has clocked up over 38 years of continuous service in London and currently works for Metroline on Route 10. Here we see RM646 outside Asda at Park Royal in July 1992, two years before being reregistered as KFF 257. The vehicle is seen on Route 226, wearing a dramatic colour scheme to celebrate Brent Council's support for the European Community. *Colin Brown*

Southend Splendour

Right: Newly repainted RM993, with the revised livery of blue instead of white around the upper windows and larger fleet name, is a sight to behold in August 1992. Starting life at Stonebridge Park in May 1962, this vehicle remained with LT until purchased by Southend Transport in August 1988. When Routemaster services ceased, RM993 went to the fledgling Reading Mainline operations in February 1994, becoming No 2 in its fleet. *Malcolm King*

No Joke

Left: Gaggs of Bunny was the unlikely owner of RM1314 for seven years following its retirement by LT in December 1986. This rural scene is at Papplewick Pumping Station on 2 August 1992 and shows the vehicle operating Route 237 to Nottingham. RM1314 was sold to Button Design Contracts of London in June 1994. *Mike Harris*

Passing the Pub

Above: This September 1992 photograph depicts freshly painted RM191 outside The Hansom Cab in Dundee. Starting life with LT in February 1960, the vehicle spent seven years with Strathtay Scottish (who re-registered it) before moving to Reading Mainline in 1994. *Malcolm King*

Hounslow Extravaganza

Left: This London United garage has a habit of spicing up its garage open days by putting visiting vehicles out on to routes. On 12 September 1992, Shaftesbury & District's RMA37, with blind apertures fitted, was doing the honours on Route 111. *Geoff Rixon*

Another Blue Triangle

Right: Not to be confused with the London area operator, this name was also found in Bootle, Merseyside, as applied to this magnificent Routemaster, RMA58. Photographed in September 1992, the bus started life as BEA No 55 and also served with BEL at Aldenham, Verwood Transport in Poole and, after sale in May 1994, with Merseyrider, Liverpool. *Malcolm King*

Colour Variation

RM910 was the only Routemaster to wear this adaptation of the Kelvin Central livery. As seen on page 74 the bus is now in another unique livery, that of Edinburgh Tramways. Kelvin Scottish (later Kelvin Central) purchased no fewer than 68 Routemasters from August 1985 onwards. *Malcolm King*

New Image

Slight variations in livery were not uncommon for Kelvin Central's Routemaster fleet but only a few carried the later red and cream colours as worn by RM321 in this September 1992 photograph. By this time the vehicle's seven-year career with this Glasgow operator was coming to an end. An optical illusion created by the camera has Colonel Sanders firmly stuck to the windscreen. *Malcolm King*

Twice Re-registered

Left: Having lost its LT registration, WLT 471, in favour of EDS 394A, following sale to Kelvin Scottish in 1986, RM471 later obtained an older registration which, in London terms, would have placed it somewhere in the middle of the RT class. Entering service in November 1960 at Hanwell to replace trolleybuses on the 607 route, the vehicle was bought from a breaker in January 1993 by Frontline Buses and is seen here in July of that year working a Birmingham local service. Subsequently acquired for preservation in October 1994, RM471 was put into LT green livery but has now been resold for private hire use, with platform doors fitted. *Malcolm King*

Bob-a-Job

Right: Currently owned by Harrogate Eagles Venture Scouts, RM757 was earning some extra money for East Yorkshire when it was photographed in Doncaster on loan to South Yorkshire Transport. East Yorkshire bought 19 Routemasters plus five for spares and RM757 was one of three painted in Scarborough & District livery. Routemaster operation by East Yorkshire lasted seven years and this vehicle was reregistered as NVS 855 in 1993. *Malcolm King*

Breaking with Tradition

Above: The takeover of former LT routes by private operators brought different liveries into the capital but prompted an edict that new operators would have to paint their vehicles predominantly red. Kentish Bus, part of the British Bus Group and one of the London Country successor companies, took over Route 19 in 1993 using 24 Iveco-engined RMLs on lease. Newly repainted, RML2548 is seen arriving at Hyde Park Corner on 7 June 1993. The route and the Routemasters have now transferred to Arriva and the buses are back in red livery. *Geoff Rixon*

Sun, Sea and Sand

Right: In contrast with its previous haunts in London and Glasgow, RM1149 experiences the pleasures of the South Coast in August 1993, working a local service to Boscombe Pier, just visible beyond Bournemouth Pier. *Malcolm King*

BOURNE - THE DEEPINGS - PETERBOROUGH
No Parking or Fuss - Take the Delaine Bus

101ᵛ Baston
Market Deeping
Werrington
BOURNE

The Delaine

RM 2059

113

ALM 59B

TO THE
MARKET

Bourne Again

Left: RM2059 is a privately preserved bus carrying the livery of Delaine, which occasionally runs in service for that company. This shot was taken in Bourne on the occasion of the first Delaine running day in August 1993 when the vehicle was operating to Peterborough. In its previous existence, RM2059 was withdrawn from Chalk Farm in November 1986 and then spent 2½ years with Southampton Citybus.
Malcolm King

Child Benefit

Right: Among the more popular uses for redundant Routemasters has been as play buses and RM1878 was certainly one of the most artistically decorated. This scene is at Canvey Island on 10 October 1993 during its 12-year stay with Wandsworth Council. The vehicle is now privately owned and living at the Routemaster Heritage Centre, Hanwell, West London.
Colin Brown

Bonnet Up

Above: This phrase has been given new meaning by former Shillibeer-liveried RM2155 following the fitting of an Ashok Leyland engine and gearbox. This vehicle was one of 41 Routemasters sold by LT to Sri Lanka in the late 1980s. This view was taken in June 1993 at Janadhipathi Mandiraya in the Fort district of Colombo. *Andy Izatt*

Soldiering On

Right: Under military surveillance, battered RM1115 passes through Galle Face Green, Colombo, in April 1993, some five years after its withdrawal from LT. Sri Lanka, formerly Ceylon, has taken vast numbers of former London buses over the years, unfortunately running them into the ground. *Andy Izatt*

49

Houdini Act

Left: This lucky bus has twice escaped the clutches of the scrapman before settling down with its current owner, Double Vision of Sevenoaks, in November 1994. This view was taken in April 1994 at Whitehawk on the Seaford to Whitehaven route previously operated by Haven Coaches until Blue Triangle stepped in, taking over Haven's services and its two Routemasters. The registration number indicates that, following withdrawal by LT, RM245 did a stint in Scotland — over six years, in fact, with Clydeside Scottish, Western Scottish and Kelvin Central. *Colin Brown*

Having a Ball

Right: This scene from June 1994 depicts RM121 appropriately decorated for a free bus service to the Wimbledon Tennis Tournament. The vehicle started life on trolleybus replacement work at Poplar in November 1959 and passed to the LT Sports Association in August 1984. In March 1988 it was acquired by the London Bus Preservation Group, for public service use. *Geoff Rixon*

Retired General

Below: Heading down the Paisley to Barrhead road, near Glasgow, is McGills 'Centenary Bus', alias RM89. This was a long-time London resident, clocking up nearly 35 years of service between October 1959 and March 1994, and was one of two Routemasters painted in pre-1933 London General Omnibus Co livery for the launch of the new London General Co in April 1989. *Vernon Murphy*

South Coast Illusion

Right: In colours reminiscent of Brighton, Hove & District buses, and adopted by South London for its operation of Route 159, RM531 approaches Lambeth Bridge in October 1994. Unaffected by a change of ownership to Cowie Group (now Arriva) in December 1994, the 27 Routemasters in question are still pounding the streets of London on Routes 137 and 159 but have now succumbed to normal red livery. *Geoff Rixon*

Showing Its Age

Left: Re-registration in the Irish Republic has made RMA26's age even more explicit than under the UK system. The 1967-built bus was originally BEA No 60 and followed the normal sequence of ownership: LT and then BEL Aldenham. RMA26 took to sightseeing in May 1992, initially with London Coaches, before crossing the Irish Sea in November 1994. *Mike Harris*

Back Home

Right: Reregistered by East Midland in 1992, this vehicle seen operating in Perth in early 1996 is much-travelled RM980. Having left London in January 1988 when sold to United Counties and progressing through East Midland, Stagecoach Perth and Bluebird Buses, RM980 returned to London in 1997, operating with Stagecoach from Upton Park. *Vernon Murphy*

In the Money

100,000 gold pennies cover RM794, one of the Niagara Falls tour buses, seen at
work in August 1995. This vehicle came to Canada in June 1992 after LT,
Clydeside Scottish and Western Scottish service. *Colin Brown*

Water Bus

Preparing to travel 'Down River' to Wimbledon with a full load of passengers is M2206, sold by LT to this Canadian operator back in 1987. This busy scene was captured on 9 August 1995. *Colin Brown*

No Bow Tie

Below: East Yorkshire Motor Services No 819 (RM1010), seen here at Scarborough in summer 1996, carries its rather sedate livery which preceded the current brighter colour scheme. After ending its LT life at Ash Grove in April 1986, the vehicle passed through the hands of Kelvin Scottish, Kelvin Central, the Mancunian Bus Co and Blue Triangle, plus a couple of breakers who, on this occasion, fortunately resisted the temptation to practise their craft. *Malcolm King*

Shut the Window

Right: All-over advertising in the late 1990s means just that: coverage of the whole bus apart from the cab. The result is a very powerful image but this starts to disintegrate if someone decides to open a window, as aptly demonstrated by RM125 outside Leeds Art Gallery in summer 1996. This vehicle started life on trolleybus replacement duties at Poplar in November 1959 and, after withdrawal by LT in May 1987, spent some years as a playbus. *Malcolm King*

Top Decker

Left: Former Green Line coach, RCL2220, displays its impressive all-over advertising, albeit at the cost of losing the lower deck for sightseeing purposes and effectively restricting the bus to fine weather use only. This vehicle was one of the London Country Routemasters which LT retrieved from Wombwell Diesels in 1978 prior to scrapping, later converting it for use on Route 149 from 1980 to 1984. It subsequently joined London Coaches' Sightseeing fleet and was converted to open top in 1991. This view was taken in Whitehall in August 1996. *Geoff Rixon*

Back on Track

Right: Sporting a new roof dome courtesy of its current owner, Timebus Travel of Watford (see page 38), RMA37 looks exceptionally well in this view at Wembley Park in summer 1997 when part of the Jubilee Tube line was closed for engineering works. RMA37's earlier career took the normal course of service with BEA, LT staff bus and then BEL Aldenham. A brief encounter with a breaker ensued in 1987 before Shaftesbury & District came to the rescue. *Vernon Murphy*

Chinese Puzzle

Apart from the cab, there is little evidence that this early ST lookalike is actually a Routemaster. RM1873 was withdrawn from Bow in 1984 and shipped three years later to Hong Kong. Its remains are seen in December 1996 outside the Peninsula Hotel, Kowloon, alongside a more recognisable ex-West Midlands PTE Fleetline. *Andy Izatt*

Lucky Escape

Sold to a breaker in 1990 but subsequently reprieved, former Hammersmith Showbus, RM81, had also worked for Clydeside Scottish, Western Scottish and East Yorkshire before heading for warmer climes in the Atlantic Ocean. Now with Cabriolet Cars of Funchal, Madeira and fitted with offside central doors (visible through the first lower deck side window), this immaculate vehicle is seen on, believe it or not, New Year's Eve, 1997. No wonder some people prefer to leave Britain at that time of year. *Andy Izatt*

Premature Ageing

Above: With its open staircase, RM388 has the appearance, from behind, of a much earlier vehicle, no doubt an added attraction when taking sightseers around York. RM388 spent years with LT, from 1960 to 1986 and then went to Kelvin Scottish and Kelvin Central before ending up with its current owner, Yorkshire Belles of Haxby. *Malcolm King*

Upholding the Image

Right: A1 means first rate and it would be hard to find a smarter vehicle than the one shown here. This joy to behold is RM560, owned by Western Buses and photographed on 26 August 1997 at Ardrossan while working alongside Volvo Olympians on the main Kilmarnock-Ardrossan service. RM560 was purchased by Stagecoach in May 1985 and is now part of its preserved fleet. *Billy Nicol*

Fired

Left: After more than seven years working for Black Prince of Morley, RM441's trips to the Royal Armouries ended. In April 1998, this vehicle, formerly with LT, Clydeside Scottish and Western Scottish, was sold to KD Travel of Rhyl, along with its two contemporaries at Black Prince. After an unsuccessful summer season at the North Wales seaside resort, the buses were again redundant. The photograph depicts RM441 bus in Headingley Road, Leeds, in October 1997. The bus has recently returned to London for preservation. *Vernon Murphy*

Great Expectations

Right: A reduction in the frequency of the services between Kingston and Epsom following the extension of the London & Country/Arriva 406 route to Crawley created an opportunity for Nostalgiabus to fill the void by operating a limited stop service, Route 306, mainly using Routemasters. Sadly, receipts were insufficient to make the service economically viable and the route lasted only seven months. However, the vehicles, including RM1394 photographed in Kingston on 22 April 1998, are still used by Nostalgiabus on local school contracts. *Geoff Rixon*

Matching Numbers

Above: With so many Routemasters in Britain now carrying registration numbers which bear no relationship to their past or present LT fleet numbers, full marks go to the Luxembourg licensing authorities for their efforts over RM1180. This vehicle was driven to Luxembourg in October 1991 for a British Trade Fair and has remained there ever since. Now privately preserved, it was photographed on 24 May 1998 when attending a Routemaster rally. *Andrew Morgan*

Flying the Flags

Right: Six foreign countries are honoured by RM1783 as an incentive to visitors to view the city of Bath from the upper deck. This vehicle was withdrawn from service at West Ham in July 1984 and moved to Liverpool where it was converted to open top. It then returned to London in June 1987, working with London Buses and London Coaches until 1995. After a year with Blue Triangle, RM1783 went to Bath in late 1996 and is seen here on 30 May 1998. *Mark Bailey*

Welsh Rarebit

Left: Strangely, secondhand Routemasters had never found favour with Welsh operators until, in 1998, KD Travel of Rhyl took the plunge and bought three, including RM2122. This bus had been owned until 1987 by LT, who sold it to United Counties. In 1992, it went to Ribble Motor Services but was not used, and then to Black Prince of Morley whose livery was retained by KD Travel. Unfortunately, the North Wales coast had a bad summer weatherwise and RM2122 was put up for sale. Here is the vehicle in September 1998 in the company of an Arriva Bristol VRT open-topper (WTU 478W). *Chris Morrison*

Adopted Londoner

Below: The only Routemasters to start life outside London were the 50 built for Northern General. This one, photographed at Marble Arch on 17 August 1998, entered service with that operator as No 2118 in February 1965. After a 13-year career, the vehicle came to the London area and has remained in service there ever since. Apart from a two-year spell with Tower Hamlets Christian Fellowship, most of its time has been spent on London Sightseeing duties, initially under the designation RMF2794 and now as RMF588. *Geoff Rixon*

Recalled for Duty

Left: RM2078 pulls away at Hyde Park Corner on 17 August 1998. Working until August 1993, latterly at Willesden, this vehicle was put into the LT reserve fleet and, rather surprisingly, was summoned, along with RM2033, to join London United's RML fleet at Shepherd's Bush in 1997. Both vehicles still have their original LT registrations and AEC engines. *Geoff Rixon*

Welcome Home

Right: Upton Park's RM1599 circles Marble Arch on 11 November 1998 as it must have done several times before in its 36-year life, but not from 1985 to 1996. During this period the vehicle was away from London doing the rounds of various Stagecoach companies: Stagecoach Perth, Magic Bus Glasgow, East Midland Motor Services, Stagecoach Perth again and Bluebird Buses. Now it has been transferred to Stagecoach London and has regained its red livery. *Geoff Rixon*

Credit to the Owner

Left: Ten years after its departure to New Zealand in December 1988, RM1660 looks exceptionally well and remarkably original for a bus still in active service. Used previously for tours between Queenstown and Arrowtown, this vehicle also acts as a mail bus, doing two 30-mile return trips in a day. *Trevor Muir*

Artistic Licence

Left: Preserved Routemasters are normally restored to an authentic livery previously carried by that vehicle. The owner of RM910 had adopted a more radical approach by pretending that his vehicle was once an Edinburgh tramcar. In its earlier life, RM910 served with LT from 1961 to 1986 before moving to Kelvin Scottish and Kelvin Central (see page 40). *Malcolm King*

Down Under

Right: Here is RM1670 in December 1998 about as far away from London as is possible. This vehicle was withdrawn from Mortlake garage in September 1982 and exported to New Zealand where, in Auckland, it is still at work. *Trevor Muir*

Showing Commitment

Left: In the early 1990s, when RMLs were being re-engined and refurbished, standard length RMs seemed to have little future in London, yet more and more are appearing as further Routemasters are required and there are no spare RMLs. RM2185 has been refurbished with Iveco engine and fluorescent lighting and now wears Arriva's Route 38 branding to demonstrate its long-term regular use. This view was taken in November 1998 outside Hackney Old Town Hall. *Philip Lamb*

All Change

Above right: This is a Routemaster, RM1288 for those not convinced, which has carried many liveries since its Aldenham rebuild with offside platform and nearside staircase, and subsequent display at the Woburn Showbus rally in September 1984. RM1288 was then despatched to the Far East with the intention of attracting large export orders from China for London Routemasters but these did not materialise and the bus was acquired by Citybus, Hong Kong in 1987. Converted to vintage open-top style in 1989, it is seen here wearing its latest colours on 28 January 1999 at Fo Tan depot in Sha Tin. *Andrew Morgan*

Helping Hand

Below right: While the successful tenderer for Route 60 was seeking an operating base and new buses, other operators provided vehicles for this route, including Nostalgiabus of Mitcham. Here we see RM1571 about to leave Streatham for Old Coulsdon on 23 February 1999. In its previous life, RM1571 was owned by LT, Stagecoach Perth (who did not use it) and two individuals. It then went to Timebus of Watford, before ending up with Nostalgiabus who used it from December 1997 to July 1998 on the short-lived 306 service between Epsom and Kingston. *Geoff Rixon*

New Look

Left: The public debut of Arriva's latest RM sightseeing livery coincided with a minor heatwave in London in Easter week of 1999 as well-patronised ERM163 pulls out of Park Lane on 31 March. This vehicle, seen earlier on page 27, has so far managed to retain its original RM identity and registration, unlike some others recently changed in the sightseeing fleet. *Geoff Rixon*

At Last

Right: Several abortive missions were undertaken before Stagecoach East London's elusive RMC1461 could be photographed in ideal conditions, helping out on Route 15. Success finally came at St Paul's Cathedral on April Fool's Day 1999. Consequently, the final and most recent view in this book features an obsolete livery, dating back to when the vehicle entered service as a Green Line coach in 1962. *Geoff Rixon*

List of Locations Illustrated

Also of interest

abc London Buses
K. Lane   ISBN: 0 7110 2596 7

abc London Transport Buses & Coaches 1948
S. Poole   ISBN: 0 7110 2585 1

Bus Scene in Colour: Preserved Buses
P. Durham & G. Booth ISBN: 0 7110 2573 1

Heyday of the Routemaster
G. Rixon   ISBN: 0 7110 2507 x

Heyday of the Bus: Yorkshire
G. Lumb   ISBN: 0 7110 2445 6

Ian Allan Transport Library: AEC
A. Townsin   ISBN: 0 7110 2620 3

Illustrated History of London Buses
K. Lane   ISBN: 0 7110 2516 9

London Trolleybus Chronology
M. Webber   ISBN: 0 7110 2528 2

How to order: These books are available from most good bookshops or mail order by calling **Midland Counties Publications** on **01455 233747 (24 hour)** quoting the reference code **BA**, your credit card details (Visa/Mastercard/Switch/Connect/Eurocard) and the ISBN(s) of the book(s) required. Alternatively, write to: **Midland Counties Publications, Unit 3 Maizefield, Hinckley Fields, Hinckley LE10 1YF. Fax: 01455 233737.** E-mail: midlandbooks@compuserve.com. Post & packing charges: - UK customers please add 10% (minimum £1.50; maximum £3), orders over £40 are sent post-free. Overseas customers please add 15% (minimum £2), 10% for £150+ orders).

For further information on Ian Allan Publishing/OPC/Dial House titles visit our website at www.ianallanpub.co.uk.

Alternatively write to: **Ian Allan Publishing Ltd, Marketing Dept, Riverdene Business Park, Molesey Road, Hersham, Surrey KT12 4RG.**

Please include an A5 sae to the value of 50p. All titles available only while stocks last.